INSECTS UP CLOSE

Honeybees

by Christina Leaf

BELLWETHER MEDIA • MINNEAPOLIS, MN

Note to Librarians, Teachers, and Parents:

Blastoff! Readers are carefully developed by literacy experts and combine standards-based content with developmentally appropriate text.

Level 1 provides the most support through repetition of high-frequency words, light text, predictable sentence patterns, and strong visual support.

Level 2 offers early readers a bit more challenge through varied simple sentences, increased text load, and less repetition of high-frequency words.

Level 3 advances early-fluent readers toward fluency through increased text and concept load, less reliance on visuals, longer sentences, and more literary language.

Level 4 builds reading stamina by providing more text per page, increased use of punctuation, greater variation in sentence patterns, and increasingly challenging vocabulary.

Level 5 encourages children to move from "learning to read" to "reading to learn" by providing even more text, varied writing styles, and less familiar topics.

Whichever book is right for your reader, Blastoff! Readers are the perfect books to build confidence and encourage a love of reading that will last a lifetime!

This edition first published in 2018 by Bellwether Media, Inc.

No part of this publication may be reproduced in whole or in part without written permission of the publisher. For information regarding permission, write to Bellwether Media, Inc., Attention: Permissions Department, 5357 Penn Avenue South, Minneapolis, MN 55419.

Library of Congress Cataloging-in-Publication Data

Names: Leaf, Christina.
Title: Honeybees / by Christina Leaf.
Description: Minneapolis, MN : Bellwether Media, Inc., 2018. | Series: Blastoff! Readers. Insects Up Close | Audience: Age 5-8. | Audience: K to grade 3. | Includes bibliographical references and index.
Identifiers: LCCN 2016057236 (print) | LCCN 2017009499 (ebook) | ISBN 9781626176669 (alk. paper) | ISBN 9781681033969 (ebook)
Subjects: LCSH: Honeybee–Juvenile literature. | Bee culture–Juvenile literature. | Bees–Juvenile literature.
Classification: LCC SF523.5 .L43 2018 (print) | LCC SF523.5 (ebook) | DDC 638/.1–dc23
LC record available at https://lccn.loc.gov/2016057236

Editor: Christina Leighton   Designer: Maggie Rosier

Printed in the United States of America, North Mankato, MN.

Table of Contents

What Are Honeybees?   4

Hive Life   8

Growing Up   16

Glossary   22

To Learn More   23

Index   24

What Are Honeybees?

Honeybees are busy workers. These insects make honey and beeswax!

Honeybees are usually golden with black stripes. They have fuzzy hairs.

ACTUAL
SIZE:

honeybee

Hive Life

A honeybee **colony** lives in a **hive**. The bees guard the hive with their **stingers**.

stinger

colony

hive

Worker bees collect pollen from flowers. They carry the dust in pollen baskets.

pollen

worker
bee

pollen
basket

They also collect **nectar** with their tongues. Then they return to the hive.

tongue

FAVORITE FOOD:

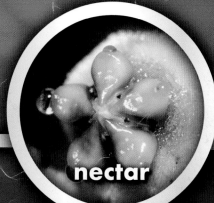

nectar

The bees make honey from the nectar. They store honey in a **honeycomb**.

honeycomb

honey

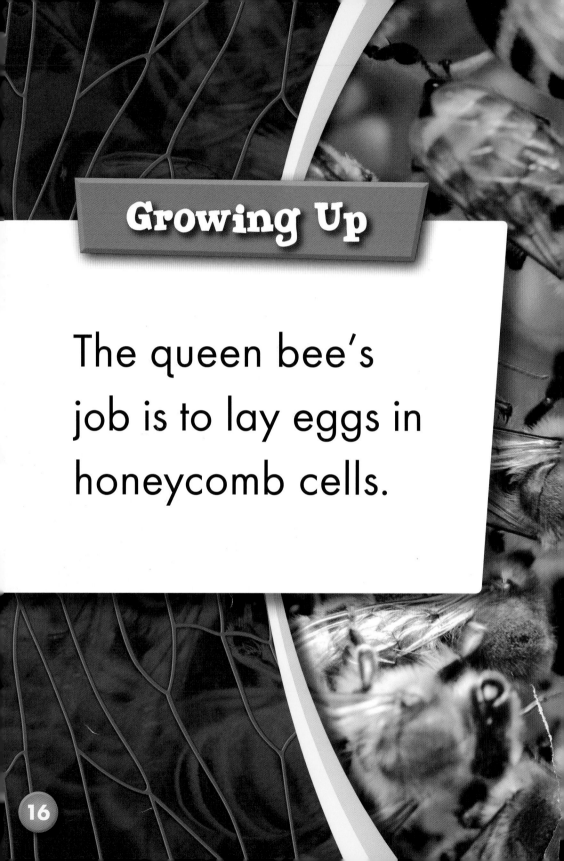

Growing Up

The queen bee's job is to lay eggs in honeycomb cells.

queen bee

eggs in cells

17

Larvae come from the eggs. Workers feed them and cover their cells with beeswax.

larvae

beeswax

Inside the cells, the young honeybees become adults. Then they chew their way out. Time to work!

WORKER BEE LIFE SPAN:

about 6 weeks

adult
honeybee

Glossary

colony

a large group of honeybees that works together to survive

larvae

baby insects that have come from eggs; larvae look like worms.

hive

a nest where a colony of bees lives

nectar

a sweet liquid that comes from plants, especially flowers

honeycomb

cells of wax made by bees to store food and raise young

stingers

sharp body parts that can release a harmful liquid called venom

To Learn More

AT THE LIBRARY

Huber, Raymond. *Flight of the Honey Bee.* Somerville, Mass.: Candlewick Press, 2013.

Marsh, Laura. *Bees.* Washington D.C.: National Geographic, 2016.

Slade, Suzanne. *What If There Were No Bees?: A Book About the Grassland Ecosystem.* Mankato, Minn.: Picture Window Books, 2011.

ON THE WEB

Learning more about honeybees is as easy as 1, 2, 3.

1. Go to www.factsurfer.com.

2. Enter "honeybees" into the search box.

3. Click the "Surf" button and you will see a list of related web sites.

With factsurfer.com, finding more information is just a click away.

Index

adults, 20, 21

beeswax, 4, 18, 19

cells, 16, 17, 18, 20

colony, 8, 9

colors, 6

eggs, 16, 17, 18

flowers, 10

food, 13

guard, 8

hairs, 6

hive, 8, 9, 12

honey, 4, 14, 15

honeycomb, 14, 15, 16

larvae, 18, 19

life span, 21

nectar, 12, 13, 14

pollen, 10, 11

pollen baskets, 10, 11

queen bee, 16, 17

size, 7

stingers, 8, 9

stripes, 6

tongues, 12, 13

workers, 4, 10, 11, 18, 21